Bigger

By Julie Haydon

Some animals are little,
and some animals are big.

oxpecker

black rhinoceros

A honey bee is little.

A honey bee lives in a nest
with lots of bees.

honey bee

A red-eyed tree frog is bigger than a honey bee.

A red-eyed tree frog lives in a forest.

red-eyed tree frog

A grey squirrel is bigger
than a red-eyed tree frog.

Grey squirrels live in forests
and cities.

grey squirrel

A black swan is bigger
than a grey squirrel.

A black swan lives in water
and on land.

black swan

A Bengal tiger is bigger
than a black swan.

A Bengal tiger lives in a jungle.

Bengal tiger

An African elephant is bigger than a Bengal tiger.

African elephants live in places where it is hot and dry.

African elephant

The African elephant
is the biggest animal
on land.